Spirit Br

TOGARA MUZANENHAMO was born in Lus parents. He was brought up in Zimbab Netherlands. His poems have appeared in magazines in Europe, South Africa and Zimbabwe, and in the anthology *New Poetries III* (Carcanet Press, 2002).

for
Irmin Durand

TOGARA MUZANENHAMO

Spirit Brides

CARCANET

Acknowledgements

Acknowledgements are due to the following: *Carapace*, *Lamport Court*, *Matchbox*, *PN Review* and *The Zimbabwean Review*.

The author would also like to express his gratitude to Lancaster Park and Arts Council England for their assistance.

First published in Great Britain in 2006 by
Carcanet Press Limited
Alliance House
Cross Street
Manchester M2 7AQ

A CIP catalogue record for this book is available from the British Library
ISBN 1 85754 852 3
978 1 85754 852 5

The publisher acknowledges financial assistance from Arts Council England

Typeset by XL Publishing Services, Tiverton
Printed and bound in England by SRP Ltd, Exeter

Contents

Captain of the Lighthouse

The late hour trickles to morning. The cattle low profusely by the anthill where brother and I climb and call Land's End. We are watchmen overlooking a sea of hazel-acacia-green, over torrents of dust whipping about in whirlwinds and dirt tracks that reach us as firths.

We man our lighthouse – cattle as ships. We throw warning lights whenever they come too close to our jagged shore. The anthill, the orris-earth lighthouse, from where we hurl stones like light in every direction.

Tafara stands on its summit speaking in *sea-talk*, Aye-aye me lad – a ship's a-coming! And hurls a rock at the cow sailing in. Her beefy hulk jolts and turns. Aye, Captain, another ship saved! I cry and furl my fingers into an air-long telescope – searching for more vessels in the day-night.

Now they low on the anthill, stranded in the dark. Their sonorous cries haunt through the night. Aye, methinks, me miss my brother, Captain of the lighthouse, set sail from land's end into the deepest seventh sea.

The Pale Saint

It all begins for Lazarus at the sound of the bell,
Late nights at the White Hart, where he met
His wife, and the girl he sees twice a week – Alice,
Whose complaints are compensated for by her huge
Smile and the wink she gives after a joke
Or when she orders a pint of ale.

Lazarus knows his way home by the feel of brick
On his palms and knuckles, his ankles rolling and buckling,
His hands following the endless wall around the corner –
Perhaps a trip or a fall; though it's less than a quarter mile
To his door, sometimes he fails to make it at all –
Not by Alice's blame, who lives a mile the other way,

But the saint's – the saint he meets lying in the street,
Needing help, always hoarse – beckoning Lazarus
Nearer. And as his head falls close to the saint's lips
Lazarus becomes warm, feels safe, until held up
By the armpits – feet dragging, and is reason
For the siren.

Nationalist Archives

1 The Mannequin's Daughter

Autumn brings a strange sense of warmth to the old buildings, the windows
filled with early evening light – auburn colours spilling over sills, flowing
onto broad sidewalks lined with tall ageless trees. Christmas will soon sour
our hearts again after bright colours darken to red roasted skins – and the fat
light of summer thins to narrow streets where shadows knelt in the snow by
the feet of those cold mathematicians of silence. There, this year simple men
will sell nuts roasted above pierced drums of hellfire, and warm themselves
by that heat throughout the winter. And here, behind a thick glaze of glass,
she stands in front of me – wearing a stunning dress of gold maple leaves. She
stares vacantly across the darkening street remembering her mother: naked,
headless and pregnant, limbs – stiff brambles rooted in the dirty snow; two
days missing, her skin as grey as birch and hard as oak. She tried to lift her
mother – holding both ankles, and after struggling for a while – realised the
absurdity of it all: a scrawny teenager on her own – her mother's body
resembling a wheelbarrow, her missing head the missing wheel.

2 The Servant Girl's Red Hat

The Minister of Home Affairs always played American music on his car radio,
Had an Austrian girlfriend and often thought of living in Krakow or Warsaw;
So it was only plausible then, that he turn right at the traffic lights – onto
The street he usually travelled when leaving the capital for his country house.

As he changed gear, he realised his chauffeur lay curled up on the back seat.
The fucker! he thought, must have fallen asleep the night before – most likely
Up to something with the new servant girl. Suddenly his driver's heavy
Snoring appalled him as the turning to the village of his country house passed.
In forty minutes they would be at the most rural border post, the guards
There could never have known his face.

All morning there had been mass suicides on a grand scale. It wasn't encouraged
But the public felt obliged to show their allegiance to the dissembled crown.
Frederic – the silent man who ran the government – personally assisted
With most of the deaths and had the Prime Minister sign each death certificate.
He also ordered all the burials to be at sea and broadcast live on state radio.

Of course the Minister of Home Affairs had objected to all this, but soon found
His wife knew much more than he did before he could go public. And after
his car
Passed through the border he kept thinking to himself as he accelerated down
The narrow country road, How careless to drive so fast and want so much so
freely.

3 Liberation

This is how water flies, whole shapes of liquid light, hovering, descending,
pulling up and taking to air – gracefully, without any immediate organic strain

*

The iris contracts for the millionth time, a vessel shooting away into quiet, a
shape vanishing into a warm journey, as fluent as water

4 The Composer

What would he make of Reykjavik – the secret dinner on his first night, or
the fishing harbour they'd pass through in a rusted truck – en route to a farm
north of the island? His head was filled with thoughts, thoughts of gunmetal
grey rocks steaming on the edges of pools, the yellow smell of sulphur, and
Hekla thawing the winter skies. But he also thought of what he'd fled from –
a whole lifetime of the unforgettable; his raw heart still developing like a
Polaroid.

For all those years in the dark he learnt how to dislocate himself from the
truth surrounding him – taking comfort in remembering an article about
Iceland's hot healing springs, the bird cliffs and nesting grounds, turfwalls
and summer midges… For years he had imagined their daylight and the
images of the island bred in his mind. And he longed for daylight, any sort of
daylight, all those days that had no end and melted into long black years of
fear.

But for now all he could think of was the city that would greet him –
where a dear friend who held no blood-questions, and had no task to ask
them, promised to meet him. They'd stay in Reykjavik for a night, have a
quiet dinner to celebrate with a family of Danes, then drive out north, and
there they'd meet with another friend who'd finally smuggle him to
Thorvald's farm – that vast quiet tract of naked land.

At the precise moment he'd begun to think of the opening words of his
speech, the phone rang. It was his wife, who immediately apologised for
calling so late. She was in her hotel room, next door to his – checking if he'd
finally managed to fall asleep. She insisted that he shouldn't stay up all night

worrying about the deer he hit and left to die on the roadside – then, after a few more words, she blew a kiss into the static line. But no words could calm his nerves. He shouted angrily down the receiver what he'd heard about and seen, how her father and the 'butchering cunts' now dealt with believers and those suspected of believing. He shouted with more conviction, asking about his siblings – had she heard nothing, nothing at all, nothing of them! Hadn't she seen what they'd done to him? How could she honestly fail to see what was truly going on!

As the hours passed he kept thinking of the island, how the winter light would suit his eyes – how the solitude would suit his soul, and most likely save his life. Having then realised he had drunk half the bottle of whisky on his own, he began to fear his incapacity for sleep, and wondered quite nervously if he'd ever make the morning ferry for Reykjavik. Then returned the thoughts of his own violent death – the shouts, the begging and pleading in the dark; all the lies he'd told his wife, all the reasons he never wanted a child; the secrets his father had hidden, the secrets instilled in him. And after a while he began to idolise the first idea of love, only to suddenly deplore it. Abandoning the whole notion with disgust, he reeled over and vomited in deep coughs of bright red blood.

His room was cold; he sat weak on the edge of the bed adjusting and readjusting the belt around his neck. The first gold moments of dawn shivered on the sea as he stared out of the window – and he thought of the long drive that had brought him here, to this town reminding him of his own childhood town – the ice-cream-coloured houses he'd run from with nothing more than his shadow in the company of other shadows – across borders, into the *freedom* of music. Whole memories of his childhood came back to him with the smell of gunpowder and the taste of warm raw liver.

But how had he forgotten Amalie, that one pure autumn, when they met everyday and watched the cold sea glimmer in the old harbour. The smell of fresh dill on her soft hands, the moles on her ankle and neck, and the smile that broke his heart entirely. How had he forgotten her, that sweet quiet hold of neglected pain.

He thought of her now, how they touched, the first time their lips met – his hands on her hips, warm on her skin and wet with the entrails of the deer, its neck craning, its wide hopeless eyes loosely rolling like ball-bearings on a velvet cloth. He remembered the expensive car steaming in the ditch, its wide bonnet curled like a harelip. Again he became unbearably nervous. And all the rubbing and squeezing of his hands could not quieten the sound of the crash nor erase the image of the young girl who sat frozen in the passenger seat; her bright red hat and screaming face already buried beneath the reflection of sky on glass.

Smoke

For a brief moment I was lost in a thought
While walking up the flight of stairs to her room –
Her hand leading me up, my eyes catching a flash
Of her bare thighs under a simple yellow skirt –

And I was a boy again, in that small moment,
Holding a present I had longed and wished for –
Bright blue emotions, sparks in mid-ignition
Bursting in my chest – lights never to grow old.

When I think of her leading me upstairs to her bed,
There's always a thought of that one precious Christmas –
The lightweight pig-iron cap-gun, the blind surprise
And spurt of gunpowder-smoke after the first bang.

The Craft

So they offered me five shillings,
And when I asked what for – they said all the dead needed to be taken in;
But I could not understand how whole fields of generations could be packed
                                        into the craft.
They assured me it could be done, and done in a matter of hours with my help;
But I stood there, all calm, barely considering it – ignoring the wind that
                                        changed,
Ignoring the terrible stench that blew into my face as they raced around me,
                                        almost panicking –
Constantly pointing to the sun to remind me time was running out;
And still I stood there, all casual beneath the craft,
Fondling its belly, marvelling at the clean shine of my growing reflection.

Six Francs Seventy-five

Each night we bought red wine from a small supermarket
Not too far from the Seine, where an overweight deaf teller
Smiled whenever we walked in. At the counter he read our lips
As we bought the cheapest wine we could find – never any change
As each time we paid, we paid the exact amount in coins you
Counted, one by one, into his open palm: six francs seventy-five.

Late in the evening you'd count up another six seventy-five
And we'd walk through the narrow streets back to the supermarket –
Fumbling through rich Parisians on their way to dinner; and you,
Who loved the city for our anonymity, became fond of the young teller
Who seemed alone and estranged and liked us too for the change
We brought to his long nights, when he read our hearts and lips.

Remember, when we figured out what he asked behind his mute lips,
'Why come twice, why not save yourselves the walk and buy four or five
Bottles in the early evening?' We laughed, as nothing would change
The way we bought or the walks we took, hand in hand, to the supermarket.
The following evening, as we paid, we looked into the eyes of the deaf teller
And said, 'It's our habit' and left it at that; and he smiled, more so at you.

From that night on – every night, this game with him and you;
He'd lift his finger and wait for the silent words to form on our lips
And we'd say, 'It's our habit'; and he'd laugh – the deaf teller –
As we played our game, and all we needed was six francs seventy-five
On those evenings near the banks of the Seine, in that small supermarket,
Always paying the exact amount, never receiving any change.

Then you left and went away, and so heartfelt was the change –
Each night I cried, and it's safe to say that he too sorely missed you.
In the evenings I still walked the narrow streets to the supermarket –
Remembering our walks in expensive coats, the jokes and your pale lips,
The way you kept the coins in a velvet pouch – the six seventy-five
That you'd always count into the soft, open palm of the deaf teller.

The night before I went away, I looked into the eyes of the deaf teller
And told him I was leaving the next day, his round face changed,
Something sad swelled in his young eyes as I placed the six seventy-five
Into his palm; he then signed to the sky, asking if I was on my way to you –
But no words this time, I could say nothing, no words of you from my lips.
I packed the bottles of wine and slowly began to exit the supermarket.

The deaf teller ran to me, tapped me on the shoulder as I thought of you,
With no change to his eyes, he shook my hand and silently said with his lips,
'It's your habit, and exactly six seventy-five'. I smiled and left the supermarket.

The Pool

1

The splashes were throngs of panic, accompanied by pleas for help – that night when all calm shattered like frozen glass. We rushed out to find father in the pool submerging himself against all resistance, wrestling with arms trying desperately to pull him out.

2

The reverend conducted the wedding ceremony before the backdrop of two lions' heads spurting water into both shallow and deep end. The first marriage in the family, where rings were exchanged and vows spoken in front of the sculpted fountains – the water falling through air, looping into the pool – as blue as truth and nearly as clear.

3

It was a concrete excavation filled with a blue cool heaven, our saviour from the heat and the long weeks of boredom; during the holidays we splashed them away, being as innovative as ever, killing time by *day-fulls*, cursing clouds till evening came.

4

Snakes dialled on its surface, in the sun, like lightning through an opal sky. Ladders of frogs' eggs failed to join everything, but hung horizontal as though the surface had a height you could climb.

At night was the music; amphibians croaking as though they sung for dear life, and as the water evaporated away the sound echoed more so, deeply – as though someone turned up the volume, gradually...

5

It also killed. When the pool was *out* – unattended, its murky green surface shone like despair. Insects, bloated frogs, bobbing rats, cordoned with thick slimy sludge around the fur, usually succumbed to its open trap. And our dog, the one we loved for years, he too was found there one morning by the gardener – afloat, a buoyant omen.

6

Now it lies empty, no one swims, no one is here to swim. The lions' heads, mounted on stone, are silent – their hollow eyes stare into the orchard where grass and weeds engulf the fruit-trees. As the sun sets the lions' heads fall in shadows into the stained empty hull where the echoes of rustling leaves can sometimes be heard.

The Laughing Wood

A rock and a river,
And on the rock a blade of sunlight intensifying the colour of moss.
The sound of water
Flowing down into the valley where they found the bags.

I have never seen a fairy,
But she professed to seeing fields of them, at play, in flight.
And to talk of them in the sparkle
Of sunlight amid the dreamy sound of water; that was a great pleasure.

The moss was warm and soft,
She lay with her head in her palm and knee up,
Exposing her soft inner thigh
As the river flowed down into the valley where they found the buried bags.

Den Haag

Deer in the park, seconds from The Hague's Central Station. *Dierentuin* was one of the first Dutch words I learned. The creatures looked so fragile and misplaced behind the wrought-iron fence, yet also strangely unperturbed as a tram reeled by – startling my father and me as we crossed the rails.

We passed a funfair, tents with bright festive lights, a miniature Catherine wheel burning out with slowing sparks – twirling to extinction, defunct and pitiful in that ending carnival.

On we walked in search of our hotel, our bags clanging and scraping at our heels, constantly searching the foreign road for a taxi. A man we had asked directions from said the hotel was within walking distance. '*Just up the road, around the corner – over the bridge and then a left*,' he said.

But up the road was confusion where time stalled and drew in our fatigued bodies as we walked searching desperately for either taxi or bridge.

Pine Thicket

There was something magical about it, the way the sun pierced through the foliage – diamond blades of amber shafting through to the soft ground bedded with pine needles.

Perhaps it was a secrecy in the shadows or the sweet sticky perfume exuding from their barks, or the way the wind slowly turned – giving a noise, through the cover, like a 'hush'.

'Come out, come out wherever you are!'

The whole grove remained deathly quiet, the bed of needles cushioned every movement. You were nearly playing the game with ghosts who did not ever want to be found.

Views without Buildings

The basil wilts near the rockery where the cactus melted back with disease,
The papaw tree falls in on itself, doubled over near the compost heap.
Heat, and the kingfisher dives to the earth,
The pair of crows shot last week still flood the yard with calls – great black
blasts of sound echoing through the trees,
The sweat of their death rising from the compost.
Last night – a dream of the jackal hobbling through the early hours, not
calling but circling a field where stumps of graves are lost in tall grass, where
shadows in the moonlight bear no claws;
The frightened jackal cowering to the wind,
Everything listening: fields of ears.
And after three calves went missing, then found the next morning all torn
apart – five jackals came across the laced meat,
The morning sun carelessly revealed them on the short new growth of grass,
on tufts of green above the black ash of last week's fire. All lay close to each
other – a true partnership of the night, pelts covered in ash, their small bodies
dunned by the blunt nocturnal end.

*

The blood-crew are always eager for the meat,
They'll find the rope and an adequate tree.
Dawn, and the axe-handler's easy with his steel –
Sharpening the blade on a wet slab of concrete.

The tether slackens when the thud cleaves the meat,
Steel meeting bone – guttural songs of a slit throat
Flushing up dust then flooding the soil with blood
As its hooves stride in the air, sky-walking to death.

And death here is as tender as the new sunlight
Or soft strips of fresh flesh twitching in a plate –
Soon skewered on a makeshift spit and placed
Over a fire. A grave is briskly dug in the distance –

Wet dust heaving out of a hole with gilded breaths,
Women busy around fires with pots of tainted steam;
For now no wailing, the blood-crew skinning the cow –
The axe-handler, axe aside, blade dulling the sunlight.

*

They have no names.
For decades and generations tractors ploughed around them,
Harvesters – rumbled their foundations. Wind and rain wiped their names
clean.
A whole family clustered beneath the evergreen shade of the karee,
Dark as night at mid-afternoon, where the odd stray cow strains its neck to
reach the leaves
In the blunt gold of a late September's harvested wheat.
No one really knows who the nameless are, and around these silent stones the
seasons pass,
And only once has anyone encountered recent visitors:
Years ago, an urban car with three elderly women dressed in mourning, and a
boy about five, drove down to the site,
All afternoon they shuffled around the headstones, picking leaves from the
tree.

Tea and Sandwiches

It's wet under foot with no paths running through the heather;
I passed a dead sheep on the peak of this moor overlooking the valley
Where the Calder flows beneath the frail cover of winter trees;
Up here, the roar of the wind fills my ears, the cold slaps my face.

Turning in the distance are the white tri-sails of a wind farm,
Strange and quiet – those tall metal ghosts writhing in unison,
Their bladed arms glinting like broad scalpels slicing the slow shine
Where the last folds of daylight ache before the gathering storm.

I've come this far with my thoughts of her losing their religion,
Our sleep separated by doors and beds, the nights' words no longer
Words, but pregnant silences long dead – the youth of our love buried
Beneath the sorrow of heavy hearts and glances that bow our heads.

A flask of tea and sandwiches; all day the walk; now I take cover
In a bird hide where the heather claws the wood. The swollen clouds
In the distance, dark gatherings of fluid, pressing their weight over
The bladed farm; the black winds splitting and spitting out this way.

The Dawn Chorus

The moon appeared at the wrong hour again,
This time it was late, startling everyone
Who stood in the attic expecting rain.
For a while there was silence, and everyone
Was troubled by the colour of their shadows;
But there was only an hour till dawn – they hadn't
Much time – so the moon's light through the windows
Was put to events becoming more frequent.

Something had to be done, they all agreed,
As the past few weeks had left their nerves heightened.
Their days were long and strange – and the need
To also fix a faulty moon frightened
Them. With dawn, the moon fell to rise with the sun,
The sky creaked, and not a song – not even one.

Roads

Perhaps the road did end up somewhere. I see it now, in the grainy
photograph she took, bending away on the southern coast of Sweden;
telephone posts linked with slack wire disappearing into the countryside
where the road turns to tufted dunes.

I hear her saying – This road leads home, commenting on shadow and
shadow turning into each other. I see her running carefree along a wild
stretch of sand, her body in full stride, the wind forcing back her hair – her
mouth caught shouting something to the camera.

Now another road leads and bends into evening. It is autumn, we decided to
take a walk. I turn to you, lost in thought – she's not here, but you are –
running in full stride, the motion streaming back your hair. I forget then start
to chase you. Your laughter, our full on laughter.

The Boy Who Ate Clouds for Tea

You shook the autumn tree and called it dusk when the leaves fell and settled at its foot. I thought, How clever of you, closing my eyes – the horizon rolling out a carpet of starlight, sleep and nothing else. How clever you had been and how much I always looked forward to your ways in ways that made innocent things from innocent things.

The following day, by the stream's bank, you shaped a breast of mud and placed a dark pebble on its summit. You put your cheek to it and lamentingly said, Earth, then made another on the opposite bank and shouted to where I stood – The flowing water should always be water! I knew then that it would be a long winter and you'd never see the following spring.

The Small Room

The men with the same face are talking all at once,
One is a theorist, another is a theorist,
The rest are all theorists.

Behind the unsealed door a masked man listens –
The sophist with club in hand,
He too is a theorist. And somewhat drunk.

What name shall I give the deaf man
Who closes his eyes and places
His fingers in his ears –
Neither wise nor foolish,
Perhaps intelligent.

He faces the outward view of the same
Street which the blind man, beneath
The balcony, has discovered and rediscovered
Over the years with his hand over his mouth.

And eyes bursting open.

The Shape of a Thousand Things

The hours pass as the night staggers through the empty streets, the cold wind whistling out of tune. In the distance, with the wrapped meat of our bloodiest thoughts, the thief of many weeks is slowly heading home.

Next door the neighbour's rows have long died down, their drunk words curdling in their throats; and while they sleep, their children lift windows and steal away into the dark with other stolen shadows.

The mind knows the bed is no resting place for grief, and fails the body failing itself upon the filth and stiffness of sweat-stained sheets.

Where hope burns blind in the blinding dark and the forceps of fear pull a black moon through the window, there is no cause, and all cause to let go.

And there are great things to be done tomorrow – but the heart keeps the broken in bed, and with the weeks that follow – there are great questions to be asked, whole words burning in the shape of a thousand things.

Skaters

The lawn was a frost-tight green waiting
For sunlight to land on its surface and turn
The temporary veil of white to sparkling dew.

After breakfast, the heavy drone of the Land Rover's
Engine warming up in the garage as children
Milled in and out of the farmhouse, still dressing –
Throwing satchels loaded with schoolbooks
Into the open back of the pickup – where thick
Blankets lay for the hour-long journey.

And we waited for the one who was always last;
The car hooting, the front door of the house wide open –
Keys dangling from the lock as he darted back again
To retrieve something else he'd forgotten.

As we waited, we jumped out of the pickup,
Ran over the gravel driveway onto the lawn –
All yells and shouts, arms held out,
The worn soles of our school shoes taking us along.

Late Night and the Road

i

From the homestead, after midnight, the faint sound of travelling trucks can be heard – droning up and down the highway. It's easy to imagine the weighted trailers hauled along the empty road; fog lights on, some yellow – others green, and a flared silver horn on the tops of the trucks, silently sucking in the wind, gathering and polishing sound for when it's blown.

ii

Drivers eating meat-pies, listening to radio shows hosting phone-ins at three in the morning, or playing games to pass the time – counting the centre white lines or cat's-eyes, trying to figure out how many pass within ten seconds or so, how many pass in a mile.

The dim-lit cockpits sometimes fill with sleep, for some distance drivers doze off then come to – to see tiny emerald globes in the roadside brush, or another truck pass with a stranger also tired at the wheel.

iii

Throughout the night the sound is amplified. Long groans trail in then haul out, the late sound of ghostlike metal expanding and contracting in the dark. The thoughts of shadows travelling on their own, along the shadowed course of the road.

*

'Amphibians for tar – fish swimming up and down the road with engine-roar in their slipstream coming off in bubbles of raw noise. Migrating fishes following the order of a path – spawning eggs in a town's belly then re-routing back to the city from where they came. Metal fish with nylon smooth scales carrying young to the creek depot where commerce hatches – the hull an empty womb of trailored iron, the lightness in return; all this to do it all again with the contract of the next season. And perhaps, a goodyear.'

Helpless Goodbyes

Through a palm print is the view of a field where a ruined
Church fosters a tree. The sound of the train's wheels
Clicks as I stare at the tree centred within the old stone walls –
Its branches spraying leaves out of two arched windows,
Its canopy neatly mushroomed, fully replacing the roof.

For a whole mile, the sight of this tree in that church,
The helpless goings away had seeded the hurt when
I stood helpless at my seat – upraised arm, palm pressed
Flat against the window, the train pulling out of Leeds.

She sat on a bench on the platform, her face – all the face
Of a face of love drawn, the train gently picking up speed.
For an hour, nothing else on my mind as buildings and fields
Morphed, as people embarked and disembarked and the morning sun
Filled the carriage with sleep. The previous night – not a wink,
Just wine and music, eyes lost like wanderers in each other's.

Laughter woke me after a station you could easily forget,
Five girls in school uniforms, no older than fourteen, stepped in,
Spoke loudly of giving head, debated swallowing or spitting.
Before then the train was running twenty minutes late, but now only fifteen –
And no real hurry, it's spring, the first drug-warm sunny afternoon
With commuters buying beers and wine from the onboard restaurant,
Reading the papers as if it were a Sunday – bodies sprawled
Over lazy seats as though they were deck-chairs in their back yards;
Jackets, jumpers, cardigans and ties everywhere like Easter palm.

The sun now pushes through the glass map of my last wave to her.
A moment ago the conductor came into the carriage punching tickets –
Now all I hear are the metal kisses of his punch through paper; the sound
Connecting with the wheels of the train on the track that fades
As I stare at the tree in the church in the field in my palm.

Excursion

All four windows open, on an empty road. Saturday afternoon – returning from a day-trip in the Eastern Highlands, the radio at top volume, the car gunning at well over a hundred miles an hour – my nephew and niece loving it all, strapped down in the back seat of the car.

School days, when I was their age on excursions, we'd chant for the bus driver to put his foot down; 'Go driver! Go! – Go! Driver Go!' each refrain gaining volume, our chants growing wilder and wilder till the bus was a vessel of screaming air.

The boys at the back stuck their heads out the windows and ate speed, had their mouths drawn dry as they screamed through the thrill. The less fortunate ones, in front or in the aisles, either thumped their fists into the upholstered seats or drummed their feet on the iron floor as the driver tested the bus's limits – inebriated by the chants of frenzied children hailing him; 'Go driver! Go!
Go driver! Go!'

I turned off the highway, the electronic windows sliding upward, cutting out the dust along the dirt track leading to the homestead; air conditioning on, the German car rolling into the garage as safe as warm honey twirling into a jam jar.

The Armchair

The fire's out, the embers grey and solid in shape – yet soft and light like air. It's now I wake in the worn hold of this armchair remembering faces all too young to know any likeness of death. These thoughts in the late hour, face after face falling into the dark; each dead portrait lost to hopeless memories framed beneath quiet glass. And tonight they come with stones, whole mobs with sticks and fire – chanting, readying to break every window of the years.

The Ornithologist's Daughter

She held papers to the conceptual republic and stood at the check-in desk with no luggage, just her papers and her ticket. She was leaving soon. A sense of family surrounded her.

Antwerp. Midwinter. I stood in a bookstore reading the large black words in children's picture-books. For days I had been standing there, going through the shelves, not really knowing what I was looking for. And although I knew all the characters in the books were dead, some of the images kept moving.

The departure lounge was full. Everyone had a seat on the flight. No one spoke. Yet she heard indiscernible voices seeping through the air as though spoken from behind a screen of warm wet cardboard. As they waited, she stared ahead, and there everyone had a *something* they saw.

I remembered I had written the book I was reading. The words on the final page were mine – as I read them I realised I knew them by heart. A member of staff asked if I needed help. I began to cry shamelessly and replied as I had replied before.

The plane prepared to take off into the night sky. She grew tired thinking of the journey. She was directed to her seat, and sat next to a polite old man who smelt of apples and tobacco with hints of cinnamon and seaweed. As the inertia of the roaring vessel hijacked her body, she fell asleep.

There were no names on the books. I felt a strong childhood longing to hear my mother read on the radio. All day I had sat by the hi-fi, intent on hearing my words read by her. At four her voice finally unwrapped from tall wooden speakers with the static sound of brown baking-paper. A story without an alphabet – scribbled on the back of a Corn Flakes box – a story of the little men and the neighbour's daughter.

Flight UV-509 went silent twenty-three years after takeoff. In a town two thousand miles off the Republic's coast, some inhabitants remember a morning when they woke to find yards and streets littered with personal belongings: toiletries, clothing, jewellery, limbs.

In Antwerp, I can still hear the trams screaming, the small wheels rolling under a tremendous weight of metal. All winter I had thought of their horses leaning over our hedge for apples. The grapevines entwined with birds. Her pink and blue T-shirt. Her milk-smile broken in half by two missing teeth.

Leaves

September comes with the thick sweeping sound of leaves and the faint antiseptic scent of eucalyptus trees lining the dirt road to the homestead.

Windbreakers, air with the sound of water crashing through their height with the force of waves – their tops peeling back, crests flinging leaves off into the wind.

*

Mountains on the lawn… mountains – great copper heaps waiting to be forked up into the wheelbarrow.

And before they were raked, before the mounds were formed, the whole lawn was a shivering sea moments before the sun sunk –

the yard, a deep old-blood colour, fissured with faint green.

*

You emerged, peeled out of the mound like a buried man parting soil for air. Who were we? We were the past of our own futures, the things that don't go away.

In those days, it was the softness of freshly fallen leaves we buried ourselves in.

*

The first leaves fell from the tops of canopies. We stood and waited, then chased after one we both agreed on as it started falling.

For hours we jostled, wrestling one another – fighting to see who would catch the most leaves. As the leaf came closer to ground – the nudging increased; we stood on imaginary stilts – budging shoulder to budging shoulder, arms in air – praying – physically reaching to god.

Whoever caught the leaf bounded and strode triumphantly, clasping it in his fist, for he knew each leaf caught was a warranted wish; each leaf straightened out and counted at the end of the day – currency, answered prayers.

Chemins Perdus

We're all dressed up in god's white suits, barefoot
And loaded. The vast white marble floor, a cold mess of shit,
Blood, urine and the last breaths of the dying.

Most here were pinioned, even after the *suicides*;
Their slippery bodies beneath our feet. And the greatest laugh is
The sight of their children serving cocktail-sausages

With mouths chattering like cold pigs. We sing,
Wondering when the women will come; but it's not that kind of party –
At the door they're handing out razor blades and condoms,

And the Angel of Death is doing his usual thing –
Calling for his overalls, to either silence or fuel the smothered screams.

The Slide

The old projector's fan hums through each guillotine changeover, and specks of dust float casually in front of the hot white light of the lens. And there I am on the wall standing with my eldest brother, T-shirt stained with all sorts of sweets that failed to make it into my mouth – thin legs bent like inverted brackets, knotted hair, and a smile like other smiles captured that Saturday afternoon at the agricultural show of '79.

A little laugh, then a memory of the stampede after the fireworks – the muscle of bodies built and plugged, stopped like cattle held in a kraal-race – the screams and cries and how all the world turned blind to my hand slipping out of my brother's – how hard and tight bodies became in the choking dust. As I called his name in the crush I heard him calling back, our voices parting further then dissolving in the panic – a panic reverberating into the years where later you would go absolutely quiet.

Thigh-high to others, squeezed helpless between crotches and buttocks, squeezed to the measure of the tightest breath. And as pain broke me to tears I thought of the last of the fireworks – all green and gold, rising with an angel's whistle to a thud like a single drumbeat in heaven. Then, the broad umbrella of light. Every head in the stadium up in awe, as my head up now staring at the picture from all those years ago, our youth static on the plain white wall.

Half Untold

On a winter's evening, outside metro Wagram,
A man lay trapped beneath the wreckage of a car.
In the cold, a crowd formed around an ambulance peddling
Blue light as firemen stood by, preparing the jaws of life.

Nothing of the man could be seen – rescuers spoke
To the wreckage as though the car itself was injured –
Its iron body, battered and ripped; and from it came
The voice of a frightened man struggling with pain

Who suddenly lifted his arm, pointed to the exit of the station
Where a stranger walked up the stairs, unaware and self-
Absorbed. All the trapped man could see from where
He lay was the stranger's face surfacing from concrete.

As the stranger passed the crowd and walked down the street,
A medic called to him, then members of the public – some
Rushed to him, guiding the confused stranger to the wreckage,
Then down to the man who lay beneath the car.

For a long time the stranger lay on the cold cobbled street,
His hand reaching out of sight – holding the trapped man's,
His face contorted as he spoke and listened with metal
Being torn apart around them. At times he cried as they spoke –

Great tears flooding down the stranger's face, big moans
Booming from his mouth – and sounds of the same beneath
The wreckage. For hours they drifted from this despair to moments
Of laughter – the stranger on his back and arm beneath the car

Laughing into the night sky, under frozen stars. Sometimes no words
As he gazed beneath the vehicle – the air holding only the sound
Of metal being stretched as onlookers wondered if the stranger
Was the one being saved, lying there, the trapped man's extension.

From the cordon, nothing could be heard of what they spoke of,
Only the sound of straining metal and sometimes a scream or a moan
From beneath the car. The crowd could only monitor the progress
Of the trapped man by the facial expressions of the stranger.

And when they finally prised the man out and freed his body,
People applauded loudly as they loaded him into the ambulance.
The siren faded, the crowd dissolved into evening sidewalk traffic,
And the stranger walked off home, drenched in blood, but well.

And when he tells the story of that night, of what he did, there is no
Mention or reference to heroes or the bold nor what was said
Between the two men that brought on their tears and laughter –
Instead, he tells half the story and leaves the rest untold.

Epworth

We folded into her arms, the soft folds of clothes over belly and breast. Two children at a time, each his own arm, each his own breast. Not too hard my boys, grandmother said, her grip unlike the grip we'd known. Her voice, tired and breathless.

Epworth, where their home was, where we'd drive each Sunday afternoon from church. From the city, off the tarred road – onto a dust strip where the landscape changed, and became decorated with balancing rocks. Some game for the gods, or something like that I thought. I could see the gods' hands peeling through the sky – picking boulders up, placing them – making towers. What else then, if not a game.

The sun was setting, that smell of gas – its hum and blue flame filters through me now. The old bookshelf by the window, closing in darkness – titles on the books' spines vanishing like words taken back. That image remains with me as she said, with my head buried into her flesh – 'I'm dying my boys'. Not sad words, just words that couldn't be taken back. Not even a mention of the disease, the growths that built and towered.

Some game for the gods, or something like that, I thought. The balancing rocks from the window's view vanishing upward into the dark. In her warm consoling hold I could hear her heartbeat, the ending of a long sweet song.

The Spirit Brides

There came the faint sound of fiddles up ahead, with the sound of the wind
                                                                                and waves,
As I rode my bicycle around a dark bend in loose snaking lines – grateful for
                                                                                the lack
Of cars on the island, elated that the stars crowned the mountains cradling
                                                                                the seaside village.

And there he stood, on the narrow road, smoking a pipe – the old man who
                                                                                flagged me down,
Who smiled and said – Are you not coming to the dance? Then pointed to the
                                                                                hall just up shore
Where music and smoky light spilt from its windows. I walked there, stood
                                                                                by one of them, peered in
And saw a whole generation of pensioners floating arm in arm above a
                                                                                wooden floor.

Nearly midnight, and though the evening air took hold of my neck, wrung it
                                                                                stiff with cold,
And probed my head – it failed to sober me up from songs of beer and ale in
                                                                                the warm pub;
And as I stared into the hall, the lights faded, the music stopped, the wood of
                                                                                the floor
Melted thick and black like smooth tar turning to night-water. To
                                                                shimmering Dutch night-water...

                                                *

Late autumn, some forgotten evening, headless brides dancing with ghosts,
The Hofvijver – still, nearly close to freezing, glistens with firelight outside
                                                                                the Binnenhof
Where Vermeer's girls gossip and peer from the windows, 'round midnight,
                                                                when the Mauritshuis comes alive –
The master's art lacing the dark with the smooth taste of virgin velvet.

No sound, nor music, only this sight of the headless gowns hovering effortlessly
Above polished water, dancing with ghosts to the wind and firelight around
                                                                                the parliament's pond.
These, these are history's lovers without faces, the youth of the ancient dead
                                                                                preserved in starlight;
Wives afloat on water – a vision of the Spirit Brides.

*

How long I had stood there is unknown. I felt a slap on my back, the old man
asking – Well aren't you coming in?
The pensioners returned to flesh again emerging from the smoky light in the
hall, still dancing
With steps of youth, past midnight – graceful and elegant, just short of a float –
Lovers locked in their lovers' arms, hoary hair flicking about like wet pepper
and salt.

Arguments Left

A whole afternoon on a section of lawn near Invalides
Where men danced awkward dances with large kites
Strapped to their waists, and bright Frisbees tossed to
Levitating dogs as lovers embraced around picnic baskets.

We lay in the sun, bottle of wine, cheeses and baguette –
Still brandishing our silences, yet holding hands as if to say,
All this at some point will pass. And the blue sky held its blue,
The men with kites still danced their awkward dances –

Swaying and swinging, heeled into the lawn by the wind;
The colourful triangles weaving quiet flight into our view.
We fell asleep, then woke in the warm twilight – where
Shapes stood stencilled in the distance, but still not a word.

As we walked back to the apartment, over Alexandre bridge,
The city lights were lit. And there, in the evening heat
We stood overlooking the Seine by a lamppost with cupids
And garlands – our stubborn silence tightening our hands.

Pallbearer

Last week he promised he'd come over and visit with his wife, that things were better as he'd taken a walk and sat in the garden that morning. I didn't believe him but smiled and in my way said I'd be expecting them. Now his coffin barely weighs on my shoulder blade, his wife thin and sickly, sits at the edge of the shallow hole that will be his grave.

We are marching him to rest. It's simple and sad things like this that need not be rehearsed, we are born to death and bred to carry its weight. I can't help but think how different he looked as he slowly approached his end: a reversal of fire in his eyes, a back-burning – as though he was being reclaimed, as though whatever he thought he had was not his.

This nearly empty casket of skin and bones and a drowned shadow beneath its sealed lid. I stumble as we walk and hear his dead body move, his bones knock against the wood. Not the knocking to enter, not the knocking for an answer – but another way to say goodbye. I take that sound with me as I drive home smelling of smoke, covered in dust, with his frail and silent wife.

Petals

From a distance, a bundle of branches, leaves and wild flowers: a makeshift hazard-sign when cars break down. A man stood directing traffic to the shoulder of the road. As drivers approached they decreased their speed – some, for a moment, stopped. On the roadside, the chaos of a gathering crowd.

As I drew in, the swaddled colours of green, pink, and brown became the uniform and skin of a child. Her head covered – a stream of blood flowing to scattered pages of a schoolbook she carried. The wind lifted and tossed the pages on the road. Some white, some red.

Monday Men

They walk through the corridors with dull eyes,
Staring heavily ahead as though all the future holds for them
Are moments of boredom and small surprise;

Room to room, with plump women at their sides –
Arms folded, mouths dumb, jumpers tugged on at the hem
By excited children wanting to see all the exhibitions in the museum:

The magic-carpet ride, the electronic games room,
And the mirrors contorting young bodies to parodies of adult forms.
The children run around these Monday men

Who wonder how all this had come to them,
Who think how they too looked in the mirrors, mothers forgotten
For an afternoon, laughing at their reflections –

Their fathers' stolid frames locked behind their backs,
On bank holidays, as they pulled faces and played games as their children
Do, mocking them in the tireless glass.

The Conductor

We stood poised, in three rows. Our breaths held in front of an audience and a man who smelt of re-lit cigarettes. His arm in the air, white glove and stick holding our voices. His head turned to the pianist, a nod, a stern look back on us – then a drop of the stick that broke our silence.

His office was a quiet dark place, like the inner chamber of an ear – your movement acoustic in every sense. You stood at his desk stolen by fear, holding your punishment slip. He did not speak, but read the note then drew a stick from a set he kept in a creel-bin, and conducted your body into position.

Man in the Bowler Hat

I am now the dislocated stranger
Stationed somewhere in your thoughts,
Dreams, or on the mundane streets you walk;

My back turned, face concealed or obliterated.
Although I am everywhere you fail to notice –
Bunched amongst myself, and alone.

I can never speak but only ever stand;
A whole legion of myself, an entire place
Of a faceless face – obstructed or draped.

Like Magritte's men I am now that clad
Man with all the inessential elements left out.

Skin-box

Each time my grandmother spoke something was retrieved from deep within herself; old words brought to light again from youth, dusty with wisdom. She breathed deeply and a hand reached into her lungs – exhaled with the hand on her tongue, supine – with recommendation, advice, or knowledge gleaming in the centre of her vocal palm.

The Red Room

Two pints of Guinness and our mastered stare out of the windows streaming with rain. Our minds lost – way past the grey shore, past the cold sea where everything's blurred in our smoke and steam. A common silence in this drawn weather, in the bar of this common hotel in this most common seaside town.

The barman's a happy fucker – yellow polka-dot bow tie, says everything's tailor-made for a laugh, has a mouth that won't stop and the luck that lets certain comments pass. But let him give that smile again, let him make another sally about us missing the bus or our hour-long wait in this red room, this dull smoke-laced red room with its strange plastic art.

Outside is where it always is for us, where our hearts have gone in vain – searching for the umpire of silence – there, where the cold rain falls on the cold cobbled beach, and the waves draw back into the sky spilling out of some deep somewhere, some unknown somewhere that prides itself in being wider than any evening, wider than anything that could conjure something darker in the dark. Outside is always where it is for us.

And what's left of the natural light streams down our faces with the pace of warm syrup. The truth is, outside, beyond the glass – no bird could ever fly in that onslaught of rain, no umpire rule against the quiet behind our lips. So we turn our pints on the mat, wait for the 352 to take us back to the station, where we'll wait for the train to take us out of this town, away from this bar, this red, red room with its strange plastic art.

But first another round and two large packets of crisps. And forget the fuckin' barman and his fuckin' jokes as the bar slowly fills with the usual local folks – the room gradually turning grey with dull conversations of an old world thick with old smoke, monotonous murmurs building to the sound of forgotten souls.

And after the hour passes, the sky and sea black as our Guinness, the town's lights come on – first in the distance, then closer – over scruffy dunes – one by one, each light flooding the town with a blurred orange fog.
                                                                    The bus arrived on time with our deflated sighs and yawns, parking empty beneath the shelter. We boarded it as it droned and waited some time for no one else to board. When the bus departed your head fell to my shoulder, my arm around you – our mastered state – both of us staring cleanly into different worlds.

Strangers

That we're not here for any short hour he comes to the car,
Leans on the roof,
And thrusts his head in through the window;
Some easy phrases between strangers you'd expect to hear in a bar.

A few questions:
How long we thought we'd wait,
The delivery –
How many litres?
What the individual rationing was,
Whether or not I thought we'd fill our cars.

All tanks here should be on '*E*' by his accounts,
And though it seems stupid that we should expect anything,
He says we'll be alright;
His own tank siphoned,
Container and hose in his boot;
Him smelling of fuel.
No questions if he's doing the hoarding-run.

He goes round to the other side,
Opens the door and casually steps in.
Picks the paper off the back seat –
Talks as he's reading.
Not a care.
Says he has a cooler-box packed with beers on the back seat of his car.
I tell him I have cigarettes.
Says his brother's a good laugh,
And brought him along for the wait.

So we sit –
And two other nameless men,
From another car,
Join us –
Doors open,
Listening to other people's radios;
Drinking,
Laughing –
As the queue slowly moves,
Snaking round the bend to the out of sight petrol station –

All of us taking our turn,
Pushing each other's cars every so often.

The first man's brother,
A travelled man,
Mentions a cookbook with recipes for whole meals prepared beneath the
bonnet of any car.
Says it's something you do on a long drive.
Harare to Nyamapanda –
A good stew with fluffy rice.
Someone mentions a journey to South Africa –
Then talk of the cricket,
The World Cup and how the boys are faring,
Then the news.
An awkward silence.
No one says what they're thinking,
Realising we're amongst strangers.
But back to simpler things,
The first man's brother tells us all about his portable four-inch television.

For a long time the cars do not move,
And like a descending flag comes sunset.
Through word of mouth we hear the petrol's all out,
And a truck has been ordered to fill up the station's tanks the next day or the
day after that.
Phones come out to call wives.
That night and two nights after that,
Blankets on back seats and packed dinners –
The days spent huddled around a portable screen the size of a fist,
Cold beers in the sun –
And no funny-talk,
Promising to get the garden done.

The Last Days of Winter

The nights unfold on flash-lit crests of waves beneath a full moon,
The wind rushes at frosted windows like the wraith of a blood bull.
Outside, a wrong step will kill you – a thirty-foot fall to the sea breathing
In coughs of rock, the waves suckling milk from the shivering moon.

I stoke the stove after a naked dash to get more logs in the evening chill,
A glass of whisky for warmth, its colour the same honeyed depth as the room
Where we stare at the ceiling, moulded in each other's arms, loaded with
                                                        laughter,
Pillow-talking on a makeshift bed of cushions in a rented seaside caravan;

As the fire dies, as the stove's light gradually lowers behind the thick grill,
A troupe of firelight flickers and dances all naked on the amber walls –
Rising up as time passes – the light finally finding itself shimmering
On the ceiling where our words had risen, unlit.

Sleep will not come tonight, and tomorrow morning's sky will be clear.
In the last true days of winter we will walk the strand, unknown to time –
Only the waves and tide laying claim to us beneath the cold sunlight.
But that is tomorrow; here the last light dies, the last dancers fall

As frost scars the windowpanes framing the milk-spilt sea, the glass
Splintered and cracked by the wind's horned rage. Now, no more words
Rise to the ceiling in the dark, just warm movements of love where
A polished sigh shoots up like a spark and bursts into the wrestle of a fuck.

Lineage

I

They came with leagues of water between them
And centuries to bargain with;
A year later, the continents were shaped –
And where Egypt ended, they lost their minds and burned every
Drug they'd taken.
Centuries later, their children woke in Brazil.

II

'IT'S THE LAST GOOD THING NOW, "TO TOUCH", BUT THE WORLD MUST
NOT BE TOLD!' He shouted, but no one then would trust Him; throughout His
youth He had always shouted, and from birth His eyes had always been
$\qquad$ bloodshot;
It was said He'd seen a forbidden future from His mother's womb.
And when the world came together again, when Egypt and Brazil were finally
intellectually linked, teachers could only prescribe His fervent sermons to
$\qquad$ soothe the faithful lineage.
His words were never taught by the human voice,
Nor the sound of artificial intelligence – only the wedding-finger of a
childless widow could point to His script in PRINT, transcribed by a male
child chosen by the state – who, by no explanation, wrote out the sermons
naked – and, until the age of thirty-six, was forbidden to step into direct
$\qquad$ sunlight.
And to say the revered one's name was blasphemy, but the thought of His
image was praised by the thoughts of thousands in the Great Hall of Mirrors.

III

Others arrived with him, through miles and miles of rain. In the northern
$\qquad$ valleys whole towns and cities would be drowned –
This city would be spared, the streets merely turned to shallow canals.
The conductor smiled. He had saved up just enough to leave the city the next
$\qquad$ day,
This was his last ride.
Shack-light upon shack-light broke his heart as the bus drove to the depot.
And when they got to the terminus and the last passengers disembarked he
$\qquad$ said goodnight with a heavy heart.
And knowing all he did about his peers, nothing could make him change his

mind, nor feel any bit of sorrow as to what would come of them.
As he walked home he whistled and began to recite the few sentences he'd
learnt in Portuguese.

Photographer

Platform four: the conductor's whistle – Amsterdam from Gare du Nord, yet you took your time – ignoring it, to take a photograph of something you'd seen. You knelt, liberated behind the lens, you – the metal and glass, your soul – an in-built negative.

*

How little you cared that the train was moving, and though I held you by the shoulder – I was afraid to wake you from that spiritual realm, where everything lay constant and still. You knelt there, on the platform, everything else forgotten – waiting to catch the light in its truth; then and only then could you return to this world. This world turning only for you and your glass eye. This world existing only to be processed, developed, then stored in metal boxes beneath the bed. And to the very last moment, our bags on the train, the train picking up speed – you held steady till you felt the time was right.

*

You were dazed, just after, like a sleeper waking from a dream – eyes unfocused, hazed and struggling to adjust. Hurriedly you placed the cap back onto the lens, jumped on the moving train, muttering something – waving excitedly at strangers in the station, delighted with whatever you had foreseen and managed to confine within your camera.

*

So that must have been it, the will to control, contort, adjust time at the whim of an egg timer. To watch faces gradually surface from treated water in red light – buildings and countrysides form from clear space to templates of black and white. A hot strength, a virility, filled your eyes as you witnessed birth in this process.

*

Once you took me to the darkroom, near the *Grote Kerke*. I watched you immerse yourself, become obsessed with the shade in a stranger's cheek – spending hours and sheets of print to get it just right. You were filled with passion and a sexual tenure as his face took form in the water, beneath a red thick sensual light.

*

We fucked passionately over the enlarger, gasping over images of ourselves drinking wine on the roof of your apartment – images living through us beneath that light that burned the paper black. In you I saw every photograph of yourself, through a mirror or delayed timer, in the blindness of a flash. You were awkward, struggling through the world – trying to keep pace with every moving thing. Trying to stop the world. How the world was made for us, and only made of art.

*

The train pulled into our stop, the sky beginning to darken over the dirty station of Hollands Spoor – our bicycles still in the racks. It felt strange that all summer it hadn't rained – the wind dry and warm, but still the sense and smell of water in the city. On our way home trees flanked dreamy canals reflecting the evening sky, we stopped near the Queen's stables and looked into the water: my communion with you, picture after picture of us rippling off the surface – all the tears we'd shed, all the laughter, all the ways of our art.

Tomorrow

Last week saw the last of the summer's heat. Tonight, the first cool drafts bring the smells of cooked dinners into the room. The faint sounds of dishes in sinks seep through the walls as children play ball games beneath street-lamps speckled with insects' wings, and the final nuances of the summer sky take time to fade.

And two screams in the shadows and shade – one of laughter, one of fear; a boy with a look of grownup avarice chases another to the bright safety of a front door. The pursuer stops not far off the threshold – winking, pounding his fist on the gate, for he knows there'll always be a tomorrow.

And tomorrow's autumn by date, handfuls of leaves have fallen, yet the air is still summer's apart from the light fostering a colder tinge when the sun sets. Ball games will stop with the oncoming pace of winter's darkness, smells of cooked dinners will be retained in safe, heated, houses; and by the gate, still pounding his fist, the runner's pursuer will wait for that tomorrow which never fails to come.

Oxygen

He had forgotten the old life and almost felt complete, here in this
intellectual cult of oxygen. One day, he thought, I will teach here –
But on this day he was determined to learn as he sat, listening.

His favourite speaker spoke, made him think of the world – and he thought
how he'd eventually change everything.
That night he burnt all his belongings, thought purely from then on, not
wavering from the texts and teachings.

At meetings they called him Cenotaph because his eyes held the fire of their
long lost dead, and the spirit of those still fighting.

Aubade

Unsaid, so it goes again, today
When I shall lay my head down
And not think of you or dream
Of you for ever till morning.

The hours pass unpromised,
Darkness will never listen or say
There, there or offer a last touch –
But stand back and wait, tainting

Every morning.

Gumiguru

I

The blue prophet blazed in the morning heat – perching silently on the fir-tree. Omen. If not omen – omega of death: the starling, stationed on the tree's top.

The rose bushes bloomed a week before, their furled petals darkening at the edges. The rain-gauge stood empty and webbed with tight blades of grass at its foot. Bees hovered above the lawn carpeted with jacaranda flowers. Foxglove and bocconia hung in the warm shade of the eaves – the baskets dripping around the house. Wasps took flight – building nests, while bulbuls swooped down, hawking insects as trees stood in the heat, waiting for the wind to blow. Each warm draft like the pant of a dog.

*

Tractor sound; hoarse diesel groans building up to the homestead. The drivers coming in for lunch, vehicles parking in shaded slots behind the sheds. Their bulk hauling up dust, the clangour of plough discs coated with red earth – exhaust fumes coughing up towers of thick cloud.

For the few minutes it took the procession to dock, the whole yard became an industrial cacophony of engine noise: the pulling-in, the revs, the shouts of drivers on their way to lunch.

And father slept through it all – curled in bed like an ancient fossil.

The starling keeping vigil.

*

How harsh the acacia field looked to the east: a lime-green forest of thorns in contrast to the distant harrowed fields. The short needle-leafed trees dominated the landscape, held no shadows – just a cruel hallucinatory effect of water flowing into a distance of dry heat.

Clumps of the hardy trees mottled the view from the window, as I looked out – past the cattle dip where my brother and I stared into the dark foetid water skinned with thick slime and dung. Past the kraal where cattle were held, then herded single file into the treated trough, where splashes of muck were coughed up on both sides: muscle struggling through the dark oil-coloured water – liquid spurting out – the beasts' bellows churning out for miles. Past the fig-tree where we found a goat's body, a makeshift spear in its belly, its nipples shrivelled hard in the dusty heat – mouth open in a yawn, revealing its brown teeth and cracked, dark tongue. There, where we vowed never to go again, where anthills towered like orange castles of blood, where light fled quick when night encroached. That place, that mysterious place that caught my eye and held our fear. The wooden spear strung with white beads, decorated with red and black cloth.

II

Where wind gave life was a sparkle in a field, a glint of blades turning, and up close – the great sound of metal rolling, chopping up air. And water, the cool sound of clear water, splashing into the reservoir, belts of shimmer dancing up – dreamily lashing white breasts of egrets perched on its edge.

He stood, broad-brimmed hat and khaki shorts, one hand on its metal frame. Four years after the rise of the new flag, the country still warm from war, he stood there – cutting the figure of perfect triumph. In the background, the tall bush stood with hints of bark lost in the thick, where faces could be made out and branches arms with arms – the sky, streaked with banners of cloud.

Sunlight falls behind him, partially shadowing his stance. Trees in the distance, caressed by a light wind, their leaves alight with reds, mauve, pinks and fawn. And he stands tall, as though he'd invented this very moment: arm out on the windmill, the blades out of picture turning with the sound of metal cutting through air.

*

What great sense of wonder they gave us, climbing to the tops near the blades – a view of pleasure mixed with peril, the distance beneath our feet.
What gods we were when we found their replicas, how high we stood, what great games for towering colossuses.

*

For hours we stationed ourselves on our bellies, blowing into windmills on the sand-coloured carpet, watching the metal sails rotate, hypnotised by the silver spin. We were caricatured clouds, full cheeks blowing westward, eastward, northward and south – the vanes performing simple magic from an exhale.
We competed to see who could turn the blades fastest – then shouted into the rotation to hear our voices cut, cut, cut… to fragments of loaded air – words sliced to coded messages, wisps of secrets.

And in our chants of nonsense I'd wish the world away, but the blades
kept spinning, only to slow to a yielding pace that broke to a halt of silence.

*

Two days he lay silent in his grand cot, diminishing. The towering figure
reduced to moments of awkward helplessness. His moist skin darkening like
the earth we could not use by the vlei, where a stream dissipated into soft
black soil, where bulrushes grew in the swale and dragonflies hovered
through the putrid smell.

Near the windmill in the east, the bog was the first place we looked when
one of the herd went astray. Its unforgiving centre held the beasts – never
letting go, drawing in their bodies with harmless-looking stipes that gripped
and took a fatal hold.

And the nights now are for fear, great gasping fields of darkness without
stars – whole hours of quicksand for the dying. Trees, souls locked to the
earth, twisted with fear. And when the nights have passed, and the mornings
come still – we ask the dawn, With what ills?

The bird keeping vigil.

III

As I turn from the window, to make my way to the door, all motion is slow
motion as though the acacia field is moving.

In a car, as a child years ago, I stare out as speed propels a different field
back: an orchard of oranges, trees in the thousands – fluorescent golf balls
hurling through green branches, backward. In the field, late afternoon, a man
labours with the full weight of a basket in his hands; he walks slowly,
dissolving like a drawn-out shadow.

Those new days, their effervescence, as we explored our new country
through every open road. Father's window rolled down, the car droning
through time – slipstreamed and warm, its white bonnet cutting through air
like a buoyant plank launching out of water.

A decade and a half on, I see the same old man shuffling through the fruit-
field. His walk, redefined, his meaning – another meaning for being there. A
man I shall know and never know my whole life as a bird crashes into the
windscreen with the diminuendo of my mother's scream.

IV

It crept with the silence of light – then, with the speed of the wind, came rushing through the night with the sound of bones snapping clean and joints popping.

The fire-bell rang, its cold vibration – solid and thick. Its tone, shivering through flesh. Its sound – filled with urgency as waves of steel panic rung off with every pound of the iron bar.

Men dressed and scrambled into the night with wet sacks, stripping branches off any tree.

*

Like a distant nightmare it came in a dream. Fire, rising from the horizon, burning on its edge: a crown for that which will raise its fiery head and fill the dreamer with its light.

At the foot of the bed it appeared: translucent, pale and heavy – garnering no fear, summoning me to where we stood out beneath the evening sky: there, it held my hand as the moon and stars orbited its head.

With a long polished claw it pointed into the night – pointing far beyond reason, intellect and memory. What lay there was uncertain yet all too clear, a colourless mud; it offered to take me there, but on one condition: I shall go forever.

The lemur rolled the moon on its tongue, sucked softly, waiting for my reply. Its breath smelt of aniseed. It said nothing and still pointed *far beyond* with its arm bridging distance – offering it all; *as easy as that, as easy as crossing*
                              Distance
& what lies beyond distance, and transgresses through all time.

Outside, tears streamed down my face – voices, and hands on my shoulders ushering me back: *But where to? Have I reached there?* or still walking back, bloody and wet – my father tucking me into the standby bed. The worn mattress suspending tomorrow indefinitely.

*

Dancers, curtains of flames – souls burning – flushing forward, pulling back – arms flinging, bodies melting in and bursting out. We stood before the dancers – faces bronze-hot, tractors heaving up – cutting fireguards behind us.

Chuff, smoke, the crackle and whistling of burning, deep in the heartland of the bush. Wet sacks and branches with seared leaves mopping up flames.

A strange dance in the wind – the fire pushing forward, men shuffling back from burning arms, then at their paces – forward, back – when the wind changed.

All night.

Dawn finally reclaimed the land as the field smouldered. The sweet smell of ash like powdered sugar beneath our feet. Tufts of grass crumbling with each step we took, our bodies torn by the effort – clothes matted to us with sweat.

All night – the dance.

*

No mirror apart from the effigy folding and unfolding in the basin. Ash in my palms, dusk-like and dusty. The bathroom, sombre – a distorted face undulating on the water as I stare clean into its depth.

Into the eye of water, within the chipped discoloured basin, his face peering back at me, his wholesome image staring from beneath the surface.

Carefully I place my hand to the reflection – lightly, so as not to cause a quiver or the slightest stir; so gently the water rises to my fingertips.

I feel his cheek, an unconscious brittle sound of stubble rustling through the air, remembering I kissed him there, upon those deep eddies of dimples whenever we parted for more than a day.

V

For two days his coffin lay in the living room, the room saturated with chants and wails, dirges and local hymns. Hosho spraying rhythm all night, the seeds and dry gourd accompanied by beating drums and the flare of a kudu-horn.

The coffin was lifted at dawn, the hearse waited in the driveway. The procession spooling out of the house like black thread, the needle the coffin. Around the household, through the yard, they carried him: through the orchard, the rose garden – past the swing, past the geyser with its metal door open, the cottage, and finally beneath the fir-tree.

The starling gone. The sky swollen with clouds.

Rain clouds.

*

Plastic anoraks were drums as raindrops thudded down on us. Each child separated by three feet of muddy earth as we dibbled a hole, placed the seed and covered.

Tynwald: a three-acre plot. The clouds had been threatening for days. A heavy, pregnant wind struggled over the field as we laboured days before. Its thick breath smelling of asphalt, wet bricks or dry tea leaves in a cup.

When the rain came, it slanted in shards shooting from the heavens; clear bolting comets pummelling our coloured anoraks. I looked to my brother doing the paces: one, two, three: hoe, plant, cover – and though the light was sombre, the raindrops took on the colours of his anorak, forming a rainbow on the arch of his back.

Father, a child's mile ahead, by the boundary of the field, turned to us, angered at our slow pace. With water streaming down his face into his bearded chin, he shouted, droplets spurting from his lips, 'The last row! Then we'll all go into the house!'

All four sons; we hoed, planted and covered till the end of the field where the road, beyond the boundary, curved to an out-of-sight solitude. And even though he had done another row and told us to go indoors, he kept going with the fuel of the future.

Out in the field where maize would sprout and the sun suck the shoots into the sky – there he laboured in solitude: one, two, three – hoe, plant, cover.

*

Death led us along its path behind the hearse. The black chariot with curtained glass. Its tail-lights blinking – two scintillating stars: two stars in the constant mirage to my father's village.

His death lead us through the dust, past barbed-wire fences – to the pencil bushes of rural reservations, through groups of donkeys, cattle and herdsmen, through villages shaded beneath the deep blood-foliage of the mupfuti.

Two stars and I follow. A slow convoy trailing. A strange heavy taste in my mouth, the compass-needle of blood guiding me on, the family grave-site steering the wheels to where earth opens up with the wet breath of death.

*

On the mantlepiece, a verdite frame: a faded photograph depicts a young couple thronged by a motionless crowd – the crowd is singing, dancing beneath the eaves of a hut where dust has risen from bare feet and is now suspended in time for ever.

She holds flowers, the bride, dressed in white. The groom is all bravado – standing straight and sturdy like a tree-trunk severed just below its first branch. The best man, much smaller than him, looks to the ground as though he consults the groom's shadow, but in actuality is only whispering a joke.

And much the same as then – he looks down now, though no joke, into the grave – a throng of dancers singing and grieving as my father's coffin is lowered into the shadowed hole. My mother throws a lily to the descending casket, and both seemingly fall for ever.

VI

In the distance, the aquamarine glare from its eyes spilt into the night of a winter field. In the cold it stood, transfixed. Dart – begins the chase. Dust rumbling, billows churning in the wake of rusted metal – the car leaking oil, a trail of black slick seeping into earth, blood of the engine dense with the coming-killing knotted into the dust. The wheels – the murderous tread rolling on into the dart and jump – the night game of death. The chase. The hunt.

Song, blood-song – hypnotism by beating drum, the heart thudding – the fog in sheets of vaporous floe inches above the road, hiding, revealing the chase around the bend. Dark blades of grass flanking the roadside, gravel sparkling ahead with the fire in the chaser's eye. Jump, jump-jump – swerve, duck – wheel, skid, turn – dust spilling out over the curve. The crush of gravel beneath the wheels. Song, dead on will. Chase. Kill.

Madness condensed to a drop of rage. Full stop of words unsaid. Speed, blank as an empty page. All the world in the nip and dip of a rabbit's tail. Kill it. Kill the noise – kill the mad drum drumming mad to the beat and rhythm of blood. This mechanism blown to chaos, feeding the mind with thought – the needle slid so cleanly beneath the skin

Dear god,
the shorn fields look so beautiful
beneath the moonlight –
a sea of blue earth,
waves of loose sheaves,
sends of silence
from what the combine harvester
shot out in chaff
and left behind;
the shredded leaves and stalks
floating through the wind.

My father is there, he stands with his back to me,
the debris falling like stars through the sky,
his body a part of the hills – blue and distant.

I call out to him from the boundary of the field
where the road echoes. He doesn't hear me.
I want him to stretch out his arms and have the chaff

float all around him. He doesn't hear me.
I want the moon and stars to rest on his palms.
He doesn't hear me; instead walks to the pickup,

gets in and drives further down, over the slope
into the field of bog – the red tail-lights
disappearing out of sight.

Dawn threatens the horizon with latent shapes
and the moon begins to dissolve –
its long dream-laced-cloak wavering in the wind.

      Stared too long. Stared. Hopelessly gasping for air. The chase still on.
Headlights. Eyes taking time to adjust again. The drumming of palms on the
steering-wheel. Song, blood-song, the beating drum – the adrenaline – this
endless road knowing no route to heaven. The bobbing scut flashing in the
headlights. The windshield fogging up. Dart – swerve. The long chase, the
short corner rushing up:

        As old as I, new beard dripping black from his chin,
dust in his eyes as he waves unperturbed,   waving and mouthing, *Good-*
bye, good-bye, good-bye
beside a tree as white and painless as aspirin.

VII

      Death took all dignity from him, through its first and final stages. His
body curled like a foetus, his eyes rolled back: desperately, infinitely, he
gurgled for breath.

      The heat drew on me as I wrestled to turn him over in his bed, struggling
to churn his weight.

One by one he would take us into his arms, cradle us for a moment, rocking us: then from his god-like strength we were flung like memories into the unsure as we were hurled up then fell and splashed into the pool.

There was a safety and imagined danger in this game; he stood at the edge of the pool like a machine manufacturing joy as we ran into his arms like components into the assembly line – to be flung into absolute completion, again.

*

Fields blurred past the car's windows, its speed tested to the limit, time and distance tampering with the road. Each bend we took – another stretch was invented, where time stalled beneath the wheels.

The rubber road stretched on, pieces of life sucked out the window to dissipate in the slipstream. What was a seven-minute drive was now a lifetime's journey; the car turning off the highway, tearing through the small town – burning the streets for the clinic.

*

Nurses on the lawn, knitting, reading magazines, having lunch, dozing in the shade beneath trees. Uniforms white as purity – their poise, a poise of pure ease.

One so easily missed it in the panic; others sat with them – staring emptily at the earth, counting grains in the sand, propped up in the shade, fading on the trunks of the trees.

The car pulled in, doors flying open before the actual stop – a throw of panic in upheld arms – only body-language through loss of words. But no one came. Uniforms white as purity – their poise, a poise of pure ease.

No weight could question my strength – my hands locked over my father's chest, his back on my stomach, his loose head, as we carried him into the clinic.

VIII

The air filled with sparkling flight, a whole field gently rising with wings. Rain had fallen, the horizon clear – the sun sinking with its red heavy light loaded with dreams. November and the first sense of real rain – flying ants taking to the air in fields where a team of tractors once worked from dawn till evening; now – hazel tufts of scattered grass and orange anthills make the landscape.

In the evening light, I stop the pickup and get out to run through the field of wings – my arms out beneath the sky streaked with an aftertaste of blood – wet soil picking up and flicking from my boots. Soon, there will be a full moon, and at first it will be blood red as the sun is now, and blunt like the crown of a stillborn.

As I run, three feathered shadows stand with shadows on open ground – the buzzards' heads nodding, twisting in the flight of the ants. Their feast, a strange, portentous dance. And dusk, dusk claims the shapes, draining them into other shapes fused with black – this field, the same field years back where all seven of us walked, having no choice but to trust the dark. The endless depth of that night – a great vault where cloud cover performed illusions through the sky: pulling the whole world in, making the whole world disappear. And in that darkness was our fear, right down to the scent of mud, our feet drudging through the bog, calls of night-birds, wild dogs and jackals piercing our hearts then withdrawing like pins out of velvet cushions.

We walked, whichever way we thought the homestead was; my father almost primal. The Land Rover stuck in the distance – a presence, a dead emotion curled up in the corner of a dream.

For days it had rained, mud caked our boots and dragged us down. The weight, with each step we took, gathered – drawing on the body with a root of gravity you had to break again and again. I feared stopping and being planted in the mud – white blind roots spreading out from my toes – knees locked, and legs stiffening.

The birds lifted to a dead tree. Monstrous wingspans flapping over new stars and planets. What had I done? All around me still the hypnotic fluttering of the ants. And in the last bits of bruised sky – silhouettes of small birds and bats – I raise my hands and fall protecting my head from a large crude shape.

The sound of the wet grass slashes through my ears as I roll through the sharpness – the field turning and trembling, I fear his gasping will stop, the loud labour of his breath cease and bring in the ultimate silence while all

IX

the ward watches as though it were a picture show starring father and son. Sweat from my face dripping into his, fingers caught to the bone between his teeth.

Breathe.

A cough in the ward here and there, clearings of throats, a word or two exchanged by neighbours in adjoining beds, spectators rolling over on sheets tanned by sweat.

He drowned in his own fluid. Sweat from my face raining into his.

All eyes on us.

*

*

The first film my father and I watched together was Steptoe & Son, in an old red-carpeted theatre. The smell of popcorn and pipe tobacco; the great casual upholstered seats that nearly lost me in their depth – the way they flipped up and had my naked knees on my chin; how I stuck my head up struggling to see the screen – and, for the first time heard an audience burst out in the dark, laughing.